WHAT THE HEART WANTS

Stories of Hope and Belonging

DIANNE GROB

iUniverse, Inc.
New York Lincoln Shanghai

WHAT THE HEART WANTS
Stories of Hope and Belonging

Copyright © 2006 by Dianne Grob

All rights reserved. No part of this book may be used or reproduced by any means, graphic, electronic, or mechanical, including photocopying, recording, taping or by any information storage retrieval system without the written permission of the publisher except in the case of brief quotations embodied in critical articles and reviews.

iUniverse books may be ordered through booksellers or by contacting:

iUniverse
2021 Pine Lake Road, Suite 100
Lincoln, NE 68512
www.iuniverse.com
1-800-Authors (1-800-288-4677)

The views expressed in this work are solely those of the author and do not necessarily reflect the views of the publisher, and the publisher hereby disclaims any responsibility for them.

Cover and text design by Kay Diamond
Author's photograph by Nityia Przewlocki

Acknowledgments:
The following essays were originally published in the following publications:
"When There are Swallows" in Earthlight Magazine Winter, 2001;
"In the Landscape of Mud" in SPA Magazine Winter, 1998

ISBN-13: 978-0-595-41558-8 (pbk)
ISBN-13: 978-0-595-85905-4 (ebk)
ISBN-10: 0-595-41558-X (pbk)
ISBN-10: 0-595-85905-4 (ebk)

Printed in the United States of America

for
the Earth

CONTENTS

INTRODUCTION	XI
IN THE PRESENCE OF BIRDS	1
FIVE-FINGERED STARBURST HANDS	9
IN THE LANDSCAPE OF MUD	15
AND SO WE DANCE	21
STARDUST	25
WHEN THERE ARE SWALLOWS	31
AN UNBROKEN LINE	39
WHAT THE HEART WANTS	43
OF THE NORTHWEST WIND	49
BENEDICTION *for Valerie*	55
ACKNOWLEDGMENTS	65

WHAT THE HEART WANTS

INTRODUCTION

TWICE A YEAR, A CHOIR OF WINGS navigates our planet. Millions of birds migrate over farmlands and cities, oceans and deserts, across highways, the tundra, and our homes. A single bird may navigate ten thousand miles to return to Arctic breeding grounds or wintering sites in South America. I can never ponder the journey of birds without feeling a shiver of mystery about the forces at work in life that are beyond our ability to comprehend.

One morning in March of 1991, during the time when the barn swallows were returning to Seattle, I sat on the couch in my living room wrapped in a chenille blanket, drinking strong Indian tea. The house was so quiet that I could hear the breath of my cat sleeping on the floor next to my feet. There was pale, muted light coming through the window and a single candle burning on the mantle above the hearth.

That morning, I was reading *The Courage to Create* by Rollo May. Leaning into the cushions of the couch with my hands around the teacup, I balanced the book on my lap. My attention was sharp; riveted by May's suggestion that courage is the capacity to move ahead in spite of despair.

I was thirty-nine years old and for three decades, I had lived inside despair: aware of my own vulnerability and the vulnerability of everything I held dear. I did not yet know how to love the world in the face of the anguish I felt over all that was being destroyed. Despair arises in people for many reasons: witnessing the clear cutting of a beloved forest, facing a crisis in their own health or losing someone they love. I first became vulnerable to despair when the threat of nuclear war reached a crescendo in October of 1962.

I was nine years old at the time, skinny and freckled and, like all the girls, I wore a green plaid uniform skirt, knee socks and Mary Jane shoes. I had heard the stories about the mushroom cloud over Japan and I understood the idea of a nuclear winter. I had learned to be as terrified as the next person by the idea of nuclear war, by the threat of Communism and even at the mention of Fidel Castro's name. It struck me that the concrete bomb shelter my father had built in our basement might protect my mother, my brother and me from these things. But it troubled me to wonder what would happen to everything else: the birds in our backyard, the trees and for that matter, my best friend whose father had not built a bomb shelter to protect her.

In October of 1962, the sky was the color of a blue jay's crest and the leaves on the sugar maple tree were nutmeg with golden yellow veins. What I wanted was to love it all. The copper and gold of it. The fragrance of burning leaves. The flocks of Canadian geese with their restless hearts. But I couldn't. I had already learned that the world could go up in flames at anytime and at nine, my heart was already armored against that pain.

Although my life had moved ahead since that time—I was successful in my profession, had moved to Seattle and was happily married—I had never thought of this as courageous like Rollo May did. In fact, when I watched myself and the rest of the world move through daily life as if everything were all right, I felt it as a kind of denial. Although the threat of nuclear war had passed, it had been replaced by other threats: global warming, species extinction and terrorism, the widening gap between those who have and those who have nothing. The same uncertainty I'd felt at nine years old about whether there would be a dependable future, still existed in me.

But on that morning nearly thirty years later, those concerns were not foremost in my mind. Totally immersed in the book, I read for hours, while the light in the living room brightened and the noises of the neighborhood—people coming and going, car doors slamming, engines starting up—fell away. As I read page after page, something began to gather in me. It was a slow movement at first, just around the edges of my awareness. But as I continued to read, it gained momentum. A sense of anticipation grew in me and I began to underline words, whole passages. I put exclamation points in the margins and wrote notes to myself. What does it mean that we shape the landscape of our mind and that our mind shapes the world we perceive? What does it mean that we can create a longed for future?

At one point, I turned the page of the book, underlined the phrase *human freedom involves the capacity to choose how we respond* and stopped. I could feel a space opening in the center of my body. The space contained a thick, palpable silence like I'd never before experienced. Then, I heard a single word spoken inside my chest. Hope.

I took a deep breath and looked out the window. There were tight green buds on the Japanese maple tree, pale blue flowers on the ground beneath and four peony bushes reaching their tender arms towards the light. It seems strange to say this now but I felt like I'd never really seen the world before and the whole garden seemed soft and hazy with color.

Then I thought: I can choose hope. I must have said this over and over like a mantra. It seemed so simple in that moment, so obvious, that I wondered why I hadn't known it before. Even that first day, I knew this wasn't a momentary understanding, something that would fade with time. I knew that if I stayed true to this one thing—choosing hope—the course of my life would change.

Each morning for the next month, I spent hours in the garden. My whole being had opened. I felt unguarded and I wanted to absorb the essence of everything. How does the wind feel on the branches of the maple tree? How does rain taste to a flower? How does moss absorb the sun? I also grew curious about the source of hope in other people's lives. Trusting something deep inside myself, I broke social taboos by walking up to complete strangers and inviting them to have coffee with me. I had never done anything like this before but something was exploding inside me. I discovered that other people did have hope and soon, I was taking notes during these conversations. Those notes became the seed for this book.

A decade has passed since that spring morning. In that time, I have come to understand that hope is not a kind of naïve optimism, some certainty about a future we can never really know. I have come to think of hope as a state of being present, of living with open eyes and an open heart—letting the pain I feel be accepted as a dimension of my love. The stories in this book have been shaped by my work in wildlife rehabilitation, by my love of the Earth and by my belief in the heart's capacity to love. I write out of the knowledge that human life is not separate from the natural world and that everything I hold dear is fragile. I write out of the belief that to love this world—with all its terror and all its beauty—requires the greatest courage. But love is our way into the future. It is our only hope.

IN THE PRESENCE OF BIRDS

Each spring, migrating shorebirds rest in the estuary at Grays Harbor, Washington before departing for nesting grounds on the Arctic tundra. Thousands of dunlins, sandpipers and russet-cloaked phalaropes wheel in perfectly choreographed aerial displays, filling the air with the music of wings. Bird watching is part of our shared history, so my husband and I make the hundred-mile trip from Seattle each year.

This year we have arrived before the changing tide calls the birds down to the rich, mudflats in Bowerman Basin, so we have opted for a walk on the beach. Drawn towards the unseen forces that shape the place, Richard walks ahead of me. I love that he will walk among the jellyfish and foam at the water's edge; wondering about the moon's position in the sky and how it is exerting its presence on the water; trying to determine the pattern in the seeming chaos of the incoming tide.

It is the species that inhabit a place that draw me, their relationship to each other, and their relationship to me. What does a ring-billed gull become in changing light? A luminous shard breaking gray sky, a dark hieroglyph against blue? What am I in the eyes of a gull? How do all the birds look, and my body, beneath the pale sliver of a moon?

As I walk through dry grass, I spot two birds swimming alongside each other about fifty feet from shore. I sit down on a piece of driftwood and focus my binoculars on them: contrasting black and white coloration, long slender necks, thin yellow bill. Western grebes. All at once, the grebes rise out of the water, dark wings lifted over their backs like angels. They rush across the surface of the bay, yellow bills aimed towards the sky. They sink back down. They rise again, rushing across the water, mirroring each other perfectly as if they have become one body. They sink back down. The grace of their movements astonishes me and I see at once why they have been called water dancers.

Richard returns from his walk bringing me a smooth, green rock. He sits down next to me, lifts his binoculars to his eyes. "The grebes are in love," I say.

The two birds face each other, bobbing their heads in unison, trilling. I long to see the color of their eyes.

On the way back to the car, I find a single white feather and tuck it into the pocket of my fleece jacket. I want to believe it belongs to a grebe.

In the late 19th and early 20th centuries, the breast feathers of grebes were used in the millinery trade to decorate women's hats. In those days, hats were adorned with arching plumes, a splash of iridescent feathers or an albatross wing. I have even seen a photograph of a woman with the entire body of a fairy tern, sprayed green and mounted to the front of her hat. Was this vanity or something more?

It has been said that the fashion of the times dictated these preferences but I prefer to believe that women wore the feathers of birds to be reminded of the beauty in the world, to be reminded of their own unquenchable desire for wings. I have to admit there's a tension in me about this. I find the idea of wearing the wing of an owl, the breast feathers of grebes, tempting.

But this practice brought whole species of birds to the verge of extinction. In the Pacific Northwest, western grebe numbers were so radically reduced that President Roosevelt gave them protected status and set aside reservations for migrating birds. What loss it would have been if his vision of the future had not included the elaborate water dance of grebes. It asks us to question our own responsibility to the future and to look at what kind of vision we hold.

As people living in the 21st century, we are so accustomed to images of war, of environmental degradation, of poverty, hunger and widespread disease that it is sometimes not as easy to hold images of what we love. And we seldom ask ourselves what might be the consequences of holding to these images of destruction? How might these images affect our own health and the health of the earth? During the years when I believed the human presence on earth would result in the destruction of life, it was easy to find images of human destructiveness, human ignorance and greed. The daily news was rampant with them. I saw death everywhere, and suffering. I held to these images because they were consistent with what I believed. The result was that I lived in a chronic state of grief, and I felt deeply estranged from the natural world. Since that time, I have come to understand that imagination is a powerful tool, as powerful as political action of any kind. Might it be that if we imagine what we love—the rush of the Colorado River, the mauve sky, the smoothness of stone—the hope inherent in those images will reverberate out into the world, nurturing our own body and the whole of creation?

There's a delicate balance in the waters of Puget Sound. Each species of bird adapts itself to an environment that provides very specific opportunities to build nests, find shelter and forage for food. Even a subtle change in these conditions can threaten the balance and disorient them.

In December of 1998, a week of fierce winds stirred the water of Puget Sound into a tumult making survival difficult for a variety of seabirds. In the course of two weeks, the Olympic Wildlife Rescue team walked the beaches gathering over one hundred exhausted, emaciated birds and transporting them to HOWL, a wildlife rehabilitation center north of my home in Seattle. Although there were a few common loons, brown pelicans and orange-billed surf scoters, the largest percentage were western grebes. I had worked at HOWL the previous summer so when the story of the rescue spread through the Seattle community, I signed on for the Saturday shifts. Two weeks before Christmas, in the darkest time of the year, the story of the rescue inspired me. In our complicated, busy world, it made a kind of simple sense to my heart.

Seabirds are not a typical resident at HOWL so for the first twenty-four hours, the staff worked around the clock to create an environment equipped to sustain them. Ceramic pools were brought in, wooden drying pens constructed and to meet the need of an ongoing supply of running water, a connection to the city's fire hydrant was established. Feeding times for the birds and administration of medication were finely tuned.

When I arrived at HOWL for my first shift, I was trained in the care and feeding of seabirds and paired with, Mark, an experienced volunteer. In the basement room where we worked, florescent lights cast a strange glow over a dozen wooden drying pens, each covered with a white sheet to shelter the sick birds. The room was humid and the air smelled of seaweed and rotting fish. I wore jeans and rubber boots to keep my feet dry as I sloshed through an inch of draining water.

As Mark and I filled eight-ounce feeding tubes with a blended mixture of fish, vitamin supplements and water, we spoke about the nests of grebes, those simple woven platforms of iris leaves, water reeds and roots often seen floating among water lilies. I spoke about how I knew these birds by the name water dancer because of their elaborate courtship ballet.

Mark and I carried the tray of feeding tubes to the first drying pen where seven grebes hunkered together for warmth. Some of the birds showed their distress by moaning like calves, others cheeped like young chicks. Lifting the first grebe, I held it against my chest and restrained its slender neck while Mark pried open the sharp yellow beak and threaded a twelve-inch feeding tube down the bird's throat. As he slowly pushed in the plunger and the fish mixture entered the grebe's body, the bird struggled to free itself, pushing its webbed feet frantically into my belly. I thought about this struggle as a good sign: despite weakness and hunger, despite frightening surroundings, this bird had not given up its instinctual wariness of humans. It still had the energy to fight for its life.

As we made our way from one bird to the next and the routine became familiar, we moved into a slow, easy rhythm with each other and the outside world fell away. I forgot about the Christmas presents I still had to buy, forgot the garden that hadn't been mulched, forgot my own hunger, which was gnawing in the pit of my stomach. That slowing down and the repetitive nature of the work allowed me to notice the physical characteristics of the grebes: the flat, black crowns of their head; their feet, the color of plankton and seaweed; the thick, lustrous plumage that keeps them afloat. But what startled me the most and will return to me in the silence of my dreams, were their eyes. Even in the darkened basement room, they shone like ruby and mandarin orange jewels.

After the first round of feeding, we gathered wet and dirty laundry, changed the feces-covered newspapers under the pens, mopped the water from the floor—our hands doing what rain and the changes of the tides would have done in the wild.

During a pause in the cleaning, we stood around eating Tortilla chips and apples. One woman spoke of volunteering at a temporary rescue facility after the 1991 oil spill in Neah Bay. Another spoke of her work at the wildlife rehabilitation center on San Juan Island; how she had massaged an orphaned fawn, an injured seal. I spoke about volunteering at HOWL in the summer, about all the songbirds that had passed through my hands. "This work has everything to do with love," I said. Then I told them that with birds my heart is unguarded. I'm not worrying about what anyone thinks of me or about whether my lipstick is smudged or the words coming out of my mouth sound foolish. The absence of those petty worries frees me to be fully present. "In the presence of birds," I said, "I am more fully myself."

On a sunny January day, brisk with cold, a group of volunteers from the wildlife center gathered at a protected inlet on Puget Sound. At our feet, nineteen cardboard pet carriers, each holding a Western grebe, sat on the pebble and brine-encrusted sand. These were the storm-tossed birds we had been caring for since early December.

Ten minutes after we arrived, I looked to my right and realized the young woman standing next to me was crying, a single tear snaking its way down her cheek, sliding down the side of her neck. Sixteen, maybe seventeen but no older, she was wearing faded blue jeans, knee-high rubber boots, an olive sweatshirt open at the neck. Her long blonde hair was pulled back from her face and hung in a tight braid down her back. As she gazed out at the water, her eyes reddened, her shoulders trembled.

I touched the young woman's arm and she answered the question in my eyes by telling me her best friend had been killed the previous day. The car she was driving rolled off the road and turned upside down. Her friend had died on impact. She told me it was hard for her to imagine how this could have happened; how someone she loved so much could be there one moment and gone the next.

I took her hand. "I'm so sorry," I said. "And I'm so glad you're here today."

She nodded towards the grebes. "I needed to surround myself with life."

When she said this, tears welled up in my eyes.

During the last decade, I have asked many people to tell me about the source of hope in their life. Most have given me practical answers—the recycling program in their city, the increase in bald eagle populations, the number of people currently opposed to war. A retired fisherman from Alaska who I spoke with over coffee and cinnamon rolls said he feels most hopeful when he teaches his grandchildren about the wind, the songs of birds, the music of streams. My brother, who works for the Ohio EPA, told me his own hope lies in the fact that the air and water quality in Ohio has improved by 80% in the last twenty-five years. But never in all of these conversations had I been as moved as I was by this young girl's living example of hope. Some would have said she was simply putting away her grief or denying her loss. But I don't think so. I believe that in staying open to life in the face of her loss, the very pain she felt became a dimension of her love.

Around us people readied themselves to release the grebes. As the pet carriers were set in a row at the tide line, camera shutters clicked and I thought about how we humans are drawn to photograph these moments of connection to the natural world. There is something we come close to, something in ourselves that we want to preserve. I know that I come close to my best self when I return a bird to the wild. It is the self that wants to live as close to life as I can, touching and being touched by the things of this world.

Twelve of us stretched plastic gloves over our hands, insurance against oiling the birds' feathers. In perfect synchrony, we opened the lids of the carriers and lifted the grebes. Even through the thin gloves, I could feel the thick buoyancy of the bird's feathers as I ran my hand down the slender curve of its white neck. Leaning down, I placed the grebe in the shallow water at my feet. Next to me, the young woman waded into the water, lifted her black and white bird and gently laid it on the Puget Sound.

The birds looked around, remembering what they have always loved: the glint of sunlight on water, the smell of brine and kelp, the wide-open space. Their eyes flashed. In black and white robes, they twirled in circles, preened. Some whistled loudly. "Cr r e ee e. Cr r e ee e."

We all applauded.

The grebes opened their wings, lifting themselves skyward.

How could hope ever fade in a world where ruby-eyed birds rush across the surface of the water, free?

FIVE-FINGERED STARBURST HANDS

Picking blackberries during the last week in August, I could smell September in the air. The morning was chilly, the alder leaves yellowing around the edges and the wildlife center was quieter than it had been for months. A red-shafted flicker called from some distance as I picked and a flock of adolescent starlings whistled and burbled in the trees. When I had a nearly full bowl of berries, a man carrying a shoebox walked slowly towards me. He was a narrow man with loose fitting clothes that hung on his body as if they were a size too large. His slightly hunched posture and the way his eyes looked downwards rather than out, made him seem humble, apologetic and shy.

He smiled, a close-mouthed smile, and held the shoebox out to me. "What is?" he asked.

I opened the lid of the box and we had a look at the small creature inside. Pink, translucent ears. Pale, quivering snout. Five-fingered starburst hands. One of night's creatures, the wood rat, creature of gutters, alleyways and dumps. The spiny trundler, the docile, adaptable one.

"It's an opossum," I said.

"Poss-um?" He pronounced the word slowly, sounding out each syllable.

"Yes. A young one."

"Oh," he said. "Young one." Then he explained that he'd found the opossum on his morning paper route. He explained that it had been lying on the side of the road. He pointed to the small nest he'd fashioned out of shredded newspaper. "Ng did right thing?"

I told him he'd done exactly the right thing and he tapped on his chest several times and smiled.

"Let's go inside," I said, motioning towards the front door of the hospital.

Inside, the veterinarian took the shoebox into the examination room to check the opossum for injury, dehydration, and disease. Ng and I sat in the lobby on aluminum chairs and I helped him fill out the admission form. I asked his full name, address, home telephone number and occupation. Where and when the animal had been found. Whether he had given it food or water. After completing these perfunctory questions, I turned towards him. I wanted to know more about this man. I am always curious about those who don't walk away, those who care enough to protect the lost and the strange in our world. This is always a choice for we humans.

Close to six thousand animals and birds arrive at HOWL each year. They have been orphaned, hit by cars, attacked by cats or dogs, poisoned. All of these creatures arrive in human hands. In the five summers I have spent at HOWL, people from diverse backgrounds have crossed my path, all in an intimately human way. I have seen a stunned couple, their shirts stained with blood, sob when a crow died they'd hit with their car. I have seen a man, his coveralls smelling of cigarette smoke, sweat and fish, carrying a laundry basket that contained two dozen seagull chicks. I have seen a solitary woman in high heels and a suit who'd stayed up all night nursing the sparrow her cat had attacked the previous day. I've seen a group of backpackers who had cut their hike short in order to rescue a downy, immature barred owl they'd found on the trail. There have been housewives in sweat pants, mothers in milk-drenched blouses, athletes, lawyers, farmers and police. The one constant among them was a sense of responsibility to the creatures that share our world.

This sense of responsibility was a way of life in my family. As a naturalist and president of the Audubon Society in our hometown, my father was often called upon to care for injured and orphaned wildlife. Rabbits, robins, opossums, cedar waxwings and squirrels often found their way to our home. During those years, our kitchen housed a special drawer filled with hot water bottles and plastic baby bottles, food and water bowls and plenty of old towels. Rehabilitating wild creatures was something I took for granted the way other kids took for granted football or summer camp.

When I was fourteen, a raccoon found its way to us. It was my grandmother's doing, really: in the summer, she provided support for the children of migrant laborers and during one of her visits to their camp, she'd encountered a young girl carrying the raccoon around like a rag doll. Its two littermates had already died of starvation, and this scrawny creature was destined for the same fate: ten ounces of matted gray fur, cloudy eyes, and limp prehensile paws. For three days, it seemed the raccoon would die but instead, the Borden's Esbilac formula we bottle-fed it along with medications a veterinarian prescribed, had their desired effect. Within two weeks, he was eating Purina Dog Chow soaked in water and climbing my bedroom curtains like they were the trunk of a tree.

Raccoons are curious, playful, social and Scooter was no exception. He liked wrestling with my father and being chased around our backyard by the neighbor's dog. He liked anything small and moveable, my stuffed kangaroo especially, but also my bra and panties which occasionally ended up outside. But even more than these things, he loved wandering around the neighborhood, digging up grubs from under the old buckeye trees and scrounging for blackberries along the ravine. Most nights, Scooter slept on our screened-in porch in a hammock my father fashioned out of an old flannel shirt but sometimes, he slept on my pillow. Many nights, I went to sleep lulled by his musical chirring and his cool, mossy paw pads kneading the skin of my cheeks. The intimacy with that raccoon shaped my sense that wild creatures are kin, just as surely as my brother was, my parents or my dearest friends. That is why I can never walk away from a creature in need of help. That is why I am so curious about other humans who don't walk away.

"Where are you from?" I asked Ng.

"Laos," he said, leaning forward in his chair. "Hmong tribe."

"Hmong?"

He nodded.

"How long have you been here, in the United States?"

"Long time. I thought would love United States city, big buildings, prosper. But was concrete and noisy. No land. No growing."

I looked out the window at the thick, cumulus clouds scudding by in the deep, blue sky. Years before, I'd read about the Hmong. They were an agrarian people who farmed in the mountainous regions of Southeast Asia. Land was everything to them. During the Viet Nam war, Hmong soldiers fought in the CIA's campaign against the Communists. But when the contested lands of fell to the North Vietnamese, the Hmong lost everything. Thousands were evacuated to Thailand, France, Canada and the United States. I even read that some

Hmong men, lost without their connection to the land, die of no apparent cause while they are asleep.

I turned towards Ng. I wanted to offer this man something, some apology for all he'd lost, some sense of understanding. But the veterinarian returned to tell us the opossum was not injured—no broken bones, no dehydration, no shock. He thanked Ng for bringing it in.

Ng smiled.

When he and I walked back outside, Ng asked what would happen to the opossum and I explained that it would be cared for along with many others and then, later, released in a woods far from the city, away from all the concrete and noise.

I paused. Our eyes met. "The opossum has been on earth for a very long time," I said. "It belongs here. It is a very strong creature."

Ng brought the palms of his hands together in front of his chest. He bowed. "May you shine of luck," he said.

As he walked away, my eyes rested on him: his bewildered gait, the lonely droop of his shoulders, the five-fingered starburst hands.

IN THE LANDSCAPE OF MUD

It was the last week in April and the night sky was swirling with snow. Fifteen other women, myself, two guides and a cook were camped on a remote mesa above the Rio Chama, 20 miles west of Abiquiu Lake, New Mexico. It was the first night of a ten-day canoe trip and as we crouched around the fire trying to stay warm, we talked about our motivations for being on this trip. Most of us wanted to slow down. We wanted a break from the hurried pace of life. One woman had recently ended a marriage and wanted to "find herself." Another said she needed to "immerse herself in the beauty of the earth." There was some talk of getting in shape and, at the other end of a continuum, talk of wanting to feel a spiritual connection to the natural world. One woman—who confessed to having never slept on the ground—cursed her luck at having gone to a travel agent looking for an adventure trip and ending up in New Mexico on that brittle and cold night.

I was there because the previous Autumn I'd visited a Jesuit monastery twelve miles up the canyon hoping to experience what I'd heard about the mystery and the innate spirituality of the New Mexican landscape. But the days at the monastery had been too long, the soup too thin, my wooden sleeping pallet too hard for me to relax. At night, I heard coyotes howling and imagined rattlesnakes slipping through the cracks in the wall: the thoughts I'd had about God were not exactly soothing. One morning after a particularly harsh thunderstorm I fled back to Santa Fe. It was on the journey back to the main highway that the wide expanse of sky, the red rock cliffs, the Rio Chama, finally drew me in.

The light was especially beautiful the next morning, golden, glinting off red sandstone cliffs, and after breakfast I walked upstream along the Chama with one of the guides. As women who love the natural world, we each had our own stories. Mine were of the birds at Nisqually Delta near my home: long-billed wrens sculpting nests lined with cattails, great-blue herons rising on invisible currents of air, emerald-crowned widgeons and red-tailed hawks. Beverly's stories were of the rivers and lakes of the world: the thunder of rapids, the gentle music of water over rocks, its fluidity, its rushing and yielding. She told me that water had taught her not to be afraid of life.

We paused to watch a dozen swallows skim the surface of the river. When we continued walking, we spoke of the earth: of how much of the living is being destroyed; of our rage, and our grief about this.

"Protecting the earth has everything to do with love," I said. "When people love the earth, they can't stand by silently and watch it destroyed."

"That's one of the reasons I became a river guide," Beverly said. "I wanted to travel, to be in the natural world and breathe fresh air. But mostly, I wanted to help women fall in love with the earth."

She paused, then continued.

"My trips are different than many. I teach women to canoe not as a way to reach a particular destination but as a way to be in relationship with all of this." She looked around at the river, the canyon, the sky.

Later that morning when we returned to camp, Beverly taught us the basic strokes we needed to know in order to canoe. In orange, rubber-soled shoes, her hair tucked into a wide-brimmed hat, she spoke about fixed-side paddling and bracing strokes to prevent capsizing. She demonstrated the J stroke—a straight stroke with a corrective hook on the end—and the backstroke. She spoke about bending at the waist, adding the strength of our core to that in our shoulders and arms. She talked us through the steps of launching a canoe and debarking. These were techniques I had learned from my father many years before and standing there, I felt sleepy and a little bored. But then something wonderful happened: Beverly launched her red canoe, nosed it into the current and began a wild flight downstream.

Words will never adequately describe the experience I had watching her. There was the spray of sea-green water, the light and the music of water rushing over rocks. There was Beverly's graceful body, her effortless movements, the sense that she had become all flesh and no bone. Watching the give and take between her and the river, the quickening and then the yielding, the pushing against and then the surrender, I felt as if she was falling into her lover's arms. The moment felt so charged and filled me with such longing, I had an impulse to turn away.

Nothing about the canoe trips of my childhood had prepared me for so much feeling. As an adolescent still uncomfortable in her own skin, canoeing had been something I never really enjoyed. There had been pouring rain, blackflies and mosquitoes, and sleeping on the cold, hard ground. There were bloody Kotex I disposed of in a bathroom dug with a spade and the freeze-dried and powdered foods my mother prepared for the evening meal. I spent much of my time on those canoe trips trying not to feel, trying to ignore the unpleasant aspects of being in my body, in the natural world. In that mood of holding out what was unpleasant, I had also not experienced the sun, the sky, the water on my skin. Canoeing had been something that required effort: something I did to get from one place to another. It had not given me a deeper connection with myself or with the earth.

Years later, as an undergraduate in Boston, I was hired to teach young girls about connecting with their bodies. I'd taught them anatomy and physiology, about the use of birth control, about a woman's right to abortion and the emotional implications of that choice. But there was always a moment in these discussions when I'd put away the condoms, the IUDs and rubber diaphragms, and tell those girls their bodies had come from love. I'd speak about sexual desire as love of life and love of the body. I wanted them to have a deeper connection with themselves than I'd felt at their age. I wanted them to be less afraid.

But watching Beverly canoe made me wish I'd understood enough to take those girls out of the classroom and onto the land. What if we were taught about love and desire by learning to open our bodies and invite the sun, the wind and the rain to brush our skin? What if we learned to touch the smooth curve of a thigh by touching stones and trees and sand? Or about the sensitivity of lips and tongues, by sipping water from moss in the hold of a shallow stream? What if we learned to be present by watching the pattern of light through trees, or listening to the stillness of snow? Perhaps our lives would not become a series of obligations, where we go through the motions without feelings for ourselves or the world in which we move.

The following morning, we broke camp and slipped our canoes into the river. Being on the Chama was thrilling.

There was the brilliant blue sky, the cottonwood trees and the crimson, rosy, blood red canyon walls. The sunlight made the water sparkle like a million diamonds and the canoes glided over the surface like silver swans.

We paddled steadily for two hours through the quick, shallow water and at around one o'clock, our destination came into sight. I had not known a landscape could be feminine until we drifted into that canyon. Everything about the burnt sienna and terra cotta walls suggested the intricate folds of a womb. Even the veins of pale umber sedimentary rock etched by wind, rain and time rose in soft, undulating waves like the curves of a woman's body. The blue-green sage, the rock formations, the cottonwood trees seemed held by the canyon walls, contained and enfolded.

Towards sunset, I walked along the river. Barefoot, wrapped only in a towel, I walked slowly, the coarse mosaic of rose quartz, sandstone and mica massaging the tender skin of my feet. The river that time of day was like deep blue jade and I walked downstream, looking for dark, red mud the texture of lotion. When I found a pool, I slid into the shallow gully, dropped my towel and sank my feet in the mud. Surrounded by walls of umber rock, my body seemed pale and fleeting and for a moment, I felt separate from it all. Wanting to be part of the landscape, I began to spread mud over the soft hollows of my face, down my neck, over my breasts and belly. The mud—more red than brown but laced with threads of green—smelled dank and alive like the leaves on a forest floor.

I had wanted solitude but in time, others joined me. They took off their clothes and sank to their knees. Muscled bodies, lean bodies, round-breasted bodies slid, slithered and slipped into the mud. Hands spread mud down the long curve of an arm, over shoulders and the sleek line of a back. Laughter erupted. Eyes shone like polished marble in masked faces. One woman beat a steady pulse on her drum. A heartbeat. The rhythm of life itself. A sound that said we exist. In the cool, dry air of evening, we rose to our feet. We circled. Spun. Stomped. Howled. We opened our arms like wings.

AND SO WE DANCE

It is morning. The fog that gathered during the night is receding like deer through the trees, revealing the blue sky beyond. Earlier, I woke to the tender hooting of great-horned owls. All night while I was dreaming, the owls were conferring with the moon, their chestnut wings sweeping silver strands of light through the spring woods.

Last evening, Richard and I joined twenty others at Pema Osel Ling, a Buddhist retreat center in the Santa Cruz mountains. The group includes people from all over the United States and Germany—midwives, therapists, consultants, builders, teachers and priests—who have come to these 54-acres of wooded land and tumbling creeks to share their pain for what is slipping away in our world.

I used to believe that the only way to live with the pain I felt about polluted rivers, about the loss of old growth forests or the threat of nuclear war, was to shut it down. I feared that my heart wasn't big enough to bear all the grief I felt; that if I opened to my feelings, I would be overwhelmed. But the suppression of those feelings resulted in a kind of psychic numbing that made colors less vibrant for me, birdsong less sweet, my loving less deep. What I now know is that when I share my fear and grief with others, and witness theirs, my heart stretches and the way is opened for more life and love to enter, more compassion and joy.

This morning before we break silence and begin the work of the day, we form a circle in the meadow, link hands and dance.

The Elm Dance, as it is named, is a ritual that extends our sense of community to include the people, places, creatures, rivers and trees of the wider world. A German woman first conceived it as a response to the dying of the elm trees in her country. Since its inception, the dance has made its way around the world: to the Aboriginal people in Australia who were defending their old-growth forests; to the people in Scotland, Germany, England and Japan. Joanna Macy first introduced me to the Elm Dance at a deep ecology workshop nearly a decade ago. The story she told then—about the people of Novozybkov and how they love this dance—made a lasting impression on me.

What I remember most about the story is that Novozybkov is one hundred miles east of Chernobyl, in the Bryansk region of Russia. In 1986 after the nuclear reactor at Chernobyl caught fire, an unusually heavy rain, bearing intense concentrations of radioactive particles drenched the towns and fields and forests of the Bryansk region. The government did not inform the people in that region that the rain was radioactive and so their memories of that day include a searing hot wind, flakes of white ash falling from a clear sky, their children running and playing in the lethal rain that followed.

Today, although most of the world no longer concerns itself about the nuclear accident at Chernobyl, the people who chose to remain in Novozybkov are living with the long-term effects of nuclear contamination. Their trees are radioactive. The wild mushrooms, the blueberries, cranberries and lingonberries in their forests have soaked up the cesium 137 in the soil. Now, the only forests these people have are the ones they paint on the concrete walls of their homes: the suggestion of woodland scenes, sunlight streaming through a green canopy, silent birds on dark limbs.

It wasn't the details of the nuclear disaster that drew me to this story. What drew me were the images of the people dancing. I could see them linking hands. I could see their bodies, strong and sturdy like the trees they long to return to. I could see their arms raising, swaying like so many branches. That so many people stayed in Novozybkov, bound to each other and to the land, moved me, but imagining their shared hope was deeply inspiring. Theirs is not hope of ever having their loss lessened, their forests restored or their children safe from leukemia and other disease. Theirs is hope of finding a way to bear the suffering they've been given. This struck me as so courageous. I was humbled by it.

And so we dance.

The simple, stately steps of the dance invite many to move with their eyes closed but I prefer to keep mine open. I want to see the emerald face of the mountain and the silent faces of the people with whom I dance. The music we dance to is a Latvian folksong. Only in your feet can you truly love your land, the woman's voice croons and I think she is reminding us how to pray.

On the last round of the dance, we call out by name those parts of our wider world we extend our empathy to. Pacific Northwest salmon. The Amazon River. The children in Iraq. The California redwoods. It is a litany that will change each morning and to which I will always add the people of Novozybkov because deep inside my body, I carry images of them dancing. As we dance, this community of others—the Russians, the Germans, the Australians and Japanese—with all their losses, all their love and longing, press into our circle.

When we raise our linked hands, the lines I usually think are there dissolve. The children of Iraq come to dwell inside me. The polluted rivers. The ancient trees. Even the meadow we dance in enters me. The rufous hummingbirds. The tender hooting of the owl. It is during the Elm Dance that I experience what has always been so: we are stronger when we hold to each other. We are all branches of the same tree.

STARDUST

RICHARD AND I HAVE TRAVELED BY MINI-BUS from Loretto, on the eastern side of the Baja Peninsula and are now walking the last three miles to the Sea of Cortez. This is a land of cardone cactus, mesquite, palo blanco trees and dried bones. We walk between soft, reddish-brown hills dotted with dried grass and lone elephant trees poking up towards the sky. It is high noon and the sun is strong. Moisture gathers on my upper lip and I gulp tepid water from a canteen. I can smell sage and wood smoke. I see lizards, turkey vultures and red birds that look strangely out of place. As we come within sight of the sea, the rocks under our feet become peach, umber and maroon and the breeze is like a delicate fabric being drawn across the skin of my arms. I see hummingbirds and orange flowers and bright yellow butterflies. There is the smell of salt water in the air.

After eating some crackers and cheese, we set out on the sea in a kayak with our sleeping bags, apples, smoked salmon, granola bars, bottles of water, chocolate, a knife, binoculars, sweaters and wool socks. The day is cloudless and we wear sunscreen, long-sleeved white shirts and wide straw hats. We paddle steadily for an hour, staying close to shore. The cliffs to our left are dark gray and black but the beaches we pass are mostly white sand strewn with pastel rocks. There are flocks of pied-billed grebes, blue-footed boobies and schools of fish so exotic they look like rainbows streaming by. Occasionally, there is the cannonball-splash of a diving pelican, but mostly the sea is as smooth as stone.

At home, I had been reading Thomas Berry's book, *The Dream of the Earth*. I was drawn to Berry because he speaks about the power of story. As a writer and psychotherapist, I have always been interested in personal stories and what they reveal about the human heart. But Berry was talking about a different kind of story. He was talking about the kind of story people live by: a story that interprets the past and guides our shaping of the future; a story that tells of ourselves and our origins and explains our place on the earth. I was struck by Berry's idea that the ecological crisis is a crisis of story. This caught my attention. I had always thought about this crisis from the perspective of human ignorance, human destructiveness and greed but I had never examined its roots. Not until reading Berry, did I ask myself about the story we in the West have lived by. I hadn't made a connection between that story and what I perceived as the estrangement between our culture and the natural world. I hadn't made the connection between that story and my own despair.

My notion about my relationship with the Earth was formed early and in the context of the Catholic Church. The story I was told as a child, I more or less believed. I believed that God created the world in seven days. From nothing, he made everything and then, he gave man dominion over it all. Our place was at the center of God's creation. We lived among other creatures, plants and trees and seas, but they were created for our benefit alone. Everyone I knew took this story literally. And almost everyone that had any influence over me believed the God of this story was to be found within the walls of a Church with its crucified Lord and its dizzying combination of incense, sweat and perfume.

Outside the walls of the Church my family attended, there were sycamore trees, rolling fields of corn, slate blue thunderclouds gathering on the horizon. There was the smell of rain, the breeze across my skin and the choir of birds at dawn. Although I had no language for it then, these were the things I felt connected to; these things felt sacred to me. But I was told this was not so. Not only was I told that the earth itself wasn't sacred but also that I was made of better stuff than sea air, the scent of roses or rain. This did not make sense to the child I was. But from an early age, I was taught not to trust my own experience or to question the things I was told.

It wasn't until I reached college that I began to question what I believed about the world. And it wasn't until I met Richard that I heard a different story. This was a story of the vast space and billions of years it took for the earth to form. The fire storms. The birth of ancient stars, our sun, the moon. The first rains. It was the story of a single element changing form and becoming life in all its infinite variety. Emerald plants moving out of the water onto the land. Redwood trees rising. Pink blossoms bursting forth. Creation still unfolding in each and every one of us. In the first years of our relationship, Richard made this story come alive in me. He took me out into the world and showed me mountains that had once been the ocean floor. He stood with me on the edge of the Grand Canyon and told me how the river had cut through the earth and exposed what had been the living surface billions of years ago. He took me to the forests and told me how the oxygen I was inhaling had so recently come from the living bodies of the trees. I loved this story with its emphasis on a community of interconnected species. And above all, I loved knowing that I was descended from the same stuff as whales and harbor seals, moss, green ferns and stone. To remember this story is why we have come to Baja, a place where we imagined we could look at, touch and feel connected to it all.

We paddle for several more hours but as the sun dips behind the hills and the sky softens to pale blue, we head for shore. We are drawn by a long strip of white sand that is held at each end by a litter of smooth black rocks. The beach, like everywhere we have passed, is deserted. Beyond the beach, there are high, red cliffs with the mouth of a narrow canyon at one end. Through the opening to the canyon, we can make out the place where the sand gives way to cardone cactus, fig trees and sage. We decide to spend the night camped there.

After pulling the kayak up onto the sand and gathering our things, we build a fire pit of stones, light a small fire using dried sage as kindling and spread our sleeping bags out onto the sand. We drink cups of cool water, eat smoked salmon and study the stars that begin to appear in the night sky.

By ten o'clock, the sky is a sea of stars. Worlds are being created above us. The fire of billions of galaxies stretches away from us through distance and time. We lay down on the slowly turning earth and mold sand into the curves and folds of our backs, the back of our thighs and calves. The air smells of salt and just beyond where we lay, the desert smells of sage, dry grasses and red dust.

Stars had their beginnings in dust. In its slow accumulation through time and over vast expanses of empty space, dust formed great swirling nebulae, galactic clusters, suns, moons, planets and stars. Our sun is one of these stars and our wet, green earth is a remnant of the dust that made it. The cosmology I rest in says that our bodies are made of stardust and everything we see has come from that very same dust: the pelicans we saw today, the whales and sea turtles, the fig trees growing against the canyon walls. Knowing this, I feel simultaneously large and very small: small because my single life is such a tiny pinprick of light in a vast universe of light; and large because I am part of a vast mystery that is still unfolding. I am not completely rid of the creation story that had me believe I was separate from all of this. It remains a place in my mind. But in my heart, I know something different. I know that we all belong to each other and to everything. And for right now, that is more than enough.

WHEN THERE ARE SWALLOWS

ONE OF THE MOST BEAUTIFUL SWALLOWS OF the mountain forests in the West sits in the palm of my hand, sleeping. It seems a miracle that I am hand to claw with a tiny bird whose ancestors emerged in our world 150 million years ago. The violet-green swallow in my hand shudders in its sleep, the feathers on its white breast rippling for an instant. When I bring it up close to my cheek, it smells of dust and the dry, sweet smell of spruce. I like to think the emerald gloss of its back and wings is a remnant of that distant star we all came from in a time when the boundaries between this swallow's body and my own were less distinct.

It was thirty-six years ago in Ohio that I first encountered swallows. Interested in attracting purple martins, the largest swallow in North America, my father built a martin house in our backyard. It was a white, green-roofed house with twelve nesting cavities perched atop a twenty-foot pole. Like all swallows, the purple martin winters in the rainforests of Central and South America. Each spring, they journey north 5,000-miles to breed in territory from southern Canada to Mexico. Many people like purple martins because a colony of those birds will eat several hundred beetles, horseflies, grasshoppers and bees each day. But I believe what drew my father was their aerial ballet, their darting, soaring and twirling, the rich gurgling of their song.

During the March thaw, my father's attention turned towards the sky, waiting for the arrival of the first scouts. Although I didn't know enough about purple martins to be attracted to them, I was drawn to my father's enthusiasm and I started watching the sky, too. When the first martins arrived, they perched atop the house, glossy heads turning from side to side, scrutinizing the neighborhood. I was eleven years old then, but I still remember how their feathers gleamed like black satin in the sun.

The day the violet-green swallow sleeps in my hand, four dozen baby swallows are in my care. Some are bald, only days out of the egg. Unruly tufts of indigo feathers sprout from the heads of the barn swallows while the rough-winged swallows are pebbled with white down around the eyes. Although I care for all the songbirds at HOWL, the swallows have long been my unequivocal favorite. Perhaps, it is the idea of their long migration that draws me to these birds. Perhaps, it is the hope inherent in their return, the reassurance I feel in the repeated refrains of the natural world.

In wildlife rehabilitation, baby swallows are difficult birds to raise because they have a high metabolic rate and must be fed every fifteen minutes for fifteen hours each day. While they are fed a thick gruel through a syringe like all the other birds, on alternate feedings they also receive live mealworms.

Kneeling on the cold, wooden floor, I fill a syringe and lean towards the first nest. Six faces as dark as ebony yearn towards me, their mouths opening like a bouquet of pale flowers. I take a deep breath, slide the syringe down the first baby's throat and slowly push in the plunger. When it is empty, I remove the syringe and repeat the process. The first bird takes three syringes before tucking its head back onto its shoulders and closing its eyes; its large, white lips pressing together give its face a look of satisfied content. I move on to the next bird. And then the next.

When I complete one round of feeding, I begin the task of cleaning the nests. In the wild, swallows build mud or clay nests lined with straw, feathers, loose grasses, bark chips and leaves. The nests I construct are less artistic but equally functional. I grab a roll of toilet paper and a dozen green, plastic strawberry containers that are stacked in the corner. I take the roll of paper and tear off a six-foot length. Holding the end in place between my thumb and index finger, I wrap the paper loosely around my hand then press this nest into one of the plastic containers. One at a time, I transfer three sleeping birds into the center cavity of the clean nest. As I do, I notice the hollow tubes of their developing feathers, a feature that has changed very little over millions of years.

For thousands of years, swallows have built their mud and saliva nests on, in or near the dwelling places of humans. Our legends are rich with images of this. My favorite legend has it be that swallows, seeking sanctuary from an innkeeper who destroyed their nests, took refuge inside the walls of San Juan Capistrano Mission in southern California. The year was 1776. At the time, Father Junipero Serra was said to be in residence at Capistrano.

I like to imagine Father Serra, pulled from sleep each dawn by pale fingers of light. Rising, he would splash cold water on his face, and then open the heavy, wooden door to the courtyard. He would breathe deeply of the morning with its salty, Pacific breeze rolling over the adobe walls. I imagine him, hands clasped behind his back and head bowed, beginning his morning prayer. Each line would have been as familiar to him as the sound of his own sandaled feet crunching on the hard, dusty ground. As I think of him beginning—Oh,

God, you are the light of the morning.—I like to imagine a part of him waiting for the swallows to awaken, a part of him that spread out in all directions like light, illuminating the dark cracks and crevices of the old mission. And I like to imagine the swallows, responding to his silent call, leaving their nests in the eaves and careening into the courtyard. In that moment, Father Serra's prayer would have become an irrepressible feeling rising from his belly and bursting from his mouth. *You, too, are the light of the morning, sweet friends.* Later, he would remember how some of the swallows flew in tight, excited circles around him. And he would smile with the memory of the tips of their wings brushing his balding head.

Since 1910, the swallows' return to Capistrano has been celebrated as a time of renewal and rejuvenation of the human spirit. Visitors from all over the world go there to witness this event. During the fiesta that is held around the spring equinox, people dress as swallows and wheel and dance in the street while the old bells of the mission toll in honor of the birds' return.

By the time I finish the last nest, many of the birds are awake and pleading for food. Their vulnerability, their complete trust of me, tugs at me so hard my eyes brim with tears. I reach for the bowl of mealworms and hunch towards the birds. Holding a pair of tweezers in my right hand, I pinch a single worm and hold it over an open mouth. But the worm squirms and writhes under the pressure of my hand and when I try to insert it into the bird's tiny mouth, it drops into the nest between two birds. I make another attempt but fail.

A parent bird would crush and masticate the worm before thrusting into the young bird's mouth. In an attempt to imitate this behavior, I use my fingernails like a beak and tear the worm in half and crush it, not one of my favorite tasks but it makes my job easier. Then, to steady the bird, I touch its mouth with the index finger of my left hand while using my right hand to drop in the now-crushed worm. This is intense work requiring concentration and steadiness and my shoulders ache from the effort. For a few minutes while the birds sleep, I slip outside and sink into the deep, moist grass in the shade of an alder.

My love of swallows was rekindled nearly a decade ago. I remember the day exactly. It was spring, in the years when I was navigating through my despair about the widespread destruction of the natural world. I lay in the backyard while Richard pruned the Red Mountain clematis. With my hands under my head, I watched him weave the tendrils of last year's growth into the denser canopy of the plant. Even though despair seemed to pin my shoulders to the ground, I remember the sun, warm on my face, and the grass, thick and spongy under my back. As I lay there, I became aware of a sweet, liquid chattering sprinkling down on me like rain. A memory from an earlier time told me these were the voices of tree swallows. I looked skyward.

A dozen of those birds hung in the air above the backyard, their bodies dark against a pale sky. My eyes swept back and forth watching their acrobatic flight as they wheeled around each other, swooping and diving towards the rooftops. One moment their movements were quick and darting and the next they soared on invisible currents of air. One bird glided into the backyard, its dark wings curved like a crescent moon.

Watching their small bodies, my own body began to awaken. Currents of feeling flitted through my chest and my belly as if their wings were brushing the inside of my body.

I began to know what I believe swallows have always known: that joy is the natural state of the heart. Lying there, I felt like crying or laughing out loud but what I found myself doing was raising my arms and shouting. *Welcome back. Welcome back.* Later, I did not know if I had been welcoming the swallows or welcoming the return of my joy.

When I return to the wildlife center seven days later, the swallows are living in a large, airy room with a screen roof open to the sky. There are sturdy maple limbs leaning against each wall, their leafy branches arching into the room. There are fronds of maidenhair fern and the slender arms of alder hanging from the ceiling like green bouquets. Today, many of the birds are eating on their own, which allows me the leisure of a slower pace. After the first round of feeding, I sit on the floor in a pool of sunlight. It is early afternoon. Many of the swallows are asleep and the atmosphere is thick with dreaming.

One rough-winged swallow alights on my left arm; its wings, a dark robe around its pale breast; its face, a reddish-brown orb. As I smooth the crown of its head and run my index finger down the curve of its small back, I feel a sense of kinship with this bird, its vulnerability, perched here at the beginning of the 21st century in this beautiful, broken world.

Just the day before, my father had told me that populations of all swallows have declined by 30–40% in the last decade. He said the responsibility for this lies in development pressures in the United States and the destruction of the rainforests in Central and South America. He said that he and my mother had noticed the decline over the last decade as fewer and fewer swallows returned to their river home each spring. Against instinct, I had tried to imagine life without swallows, tried to imagine a world in which swallows did not exist. But when I did, I felt an aching loneliness and a desire to armor my heart. Hope is rarely kindled in me when my heart is armored. It thrives instead in the small moments of daily life when I work to create the future I long for, a future where the children of all species are protected, a future filled with love.

Settling the rough-winged swallow on a branch, I begin to feed the other birds. As I walk around the room, I pray. I pray silently, an ancient Buddhist prayer that in the past, has strengthened my heart. *May you be filled with loving kindness.* Each time I touch a tender head or drop a worm into an open mouth, I repeat a phrase. *May you be whole.* But today the practice is difficult. The words feel empty, the grim statistics of the swallows' decline crowd my mind and my heart is sad. But I keep at it. *May you be peaceful and at ease.*

I walk in slow motion, hoping that a slowed-down body will also slow down my mind. I pay attention to each foot, the way it plants itself on the dry ground, knees bending, hips moving through the air. I observe the birds and bless each one of them: their indigo, nutmeg, pale brown heads. *May you be happy.* But still my mind reels.

I take a deep breath and decide to pray out loud. *May you be filled with loving kindness.* I pray from every cell in my body; not just from my heart but from my arms and legs, my hands and my belly. I consciously imbue each line of the prayer with all the love I feel for these birds. *May you be whole.*

Over the next hour, I notice a change in myself. My mind quiets, my sorrow fades and gradually, all that remains is the moment I occupy now. I can hear the muted voices of other volunteers; can smell dust and the dry, sweet smell of spruce. There is the sunlight on my arms and above all else, there is the simple movement of love.

AN UNBROKEN LINE

WHEN MORNING COMES TO PRINCE WILLIAM SOUND, the pine forests shimmer with blue mist, clear fjords sparkle between steep emerald headlands and vast ice fields burn with the fire of the sun. Along the rocky shorelines salmon pour. Shorebirds, whales and harbor seals gather. And in the darkness of old-growth forests, marbled murrelets nest in the hollow cavities of trees. This is a place where the process of creation—with its endings and beginnings—is still visible to the human eye. Glacier-ground dust from the mountains becomes part of the soil, nourishing the plants and the deep roots of the trees. In their living and dying, these plants nourish the creatures inhabiting the place whom in turn, surrender their lives so that others might live.

Prince William Sound is also a place that suffered one of the most damaging ecological crises in history. In 1989, the oil tanker Exxon Valdez ran aground on the jagged shoals of Bligh Reef. Forty thousand tons of purple-brown oil spread along 1,500 miles of remote coastline. Wind-driven waves hurled oil into the trees. It is estimated that 240,000 seabirds were lost. Five thousand sea otters. Three hundred harbor seals. Twenty-two killer whales. Two hundred bald eagles. The herring population—a subsistence resource for the Native people—crashed.

All these years later, Prince William Sound is still waiting to heal. Of the dozens of species affected, only the bald eagle has recovered and I have been told that in some remote marshes, a footstep still draws an oily sheen. And we humans are waiting. We are waiting for the perceived separation between us and the natural world to heal. Stories swirl around us of our greed, of our responsibility in the destruction of the planet, of how our footsteps have eroded the fabric of life. The shadow of Prince William Sound and other ecological disasters hovers over our heads, settles into our hearts. We grieve. We are lonely.

And yet for all the horror and ignorance made evident by these crises, what they also reveal is our capacity to love. That week in Valdez, for instance, the population doubled as rescue crews, wildlife biologists, oil cleanup specialists and just regular folks arrived. There were cars, trucks and Volkswagen vans parked along the shoulder of every road. People had driven five hundred miles, seven hundred and fifty miles, to be there. Some had flown in from Seattle, from Chicago, from Washington D.C. Some came because they were trained specialists. Others came simply because they loved the Sound and could not stay away.

In one parking lot, a food service truck sat surrounded by people drinking coffee out of Styrofoam cups. The woman working there was from Anchorage. She was heavy set, with close-cropped silver hair that stood up on top. She had kayaked on the Sound every summer in her childhood. She wanted to help out, she said, but she knew she wasn't up for physical labor. Besides giving away the coffee, she had started a blanket collection for all the people sleeping on the Church floor.

It was Easter Sunday and in one of the parks, wildlife rescue volunteers held an impromptu service. They stood in a close circle and someone recited a W.S. Merwin poem. *With the animals dying around us, we are saying thank you.* Then a man wearing a red plaid cap with the earflaps down began to sing Amazing Grace. Someone else lit a votive candle in a glass jar, a white candle that smoked and smelled of vanilla. Afterwards, they stood in silence. Some of them cried into their open palms.

All these stories live within me but there is one story from that week that lives more deeply in me than the rest. I read it in the daily journal that was kept by the Coast Guard and later made available to the public. Among all the other entries about high winds, about otter pups born to oiled mothers, about bald eagles feasting on oiled fish, this one story captured my imagination. It is the story of one hundred men and women who wiped oil from the north side of Green Island. In the face of thousands of gallons of oil, those men and women had no cleanup equipment, no bulldozers, no hoses or hot water, no biochemical treatment. All they had were their bare hands. I could not put this story from my mind and for months, I contemplated the reason for this.

When I think of that scene, now, as I have dozens of times, I imagine a low fog, mist rising upward like rain in reverse, a foghorn, perhaps the clang of bells in the distance. There is the faint smell of salt, the more potent stench of oil, the smell of human sweat. There are the human bodies. The slow ache in shoulders as the men and women bend under their labor. There are the thrumming hearts, the blood rushing through translucent veins, the lungs taking in air recently exhaled from the bodies of cedar trees. And then there are the hands, such vulnerable instruments, those organs of touching, with thin skin and pale blue veins, tender, naked like baby birds. I think of those hands and remember they were fins hundreds of millions of years ago and again in this life, in their mothers' womb. They are hands full of the life they have known, including the touch of all they have loved. Nearly four billion years of evolution are in those hands. The ancestors are there: ancestors who climbed and reached and grasped; ancestors who found their way to gather seeds and plant them, to weave baskets, to make fire, to draw on the stone walls of caves.

All of the life in those bodies, all of the evolutionary history, all of the earth itself is present in those hands wiping oil from rocks and tidal pools and sand. The single element from which all of life has come is there. The mountains and oceans, rock and stone and sand are there; the sky rolling with thunder; the rain that has been drenching the earth for more than four billion years. Everything is there in that labor. It is an unbroken line, to who we are and what we are connected to. When we remember this connection, the whole world wakes up. The stars applaud. All of creation sighs.

WHAT THE HEART WANTS

I AM WALKING THE FIVE-MILE LOOP TRAIL AT Nisqually Delta, concentrating on my bare feet touching the dirt, the pieces of bark, twigs and dried grass, how the earth feels beneath me, solid, moist, alive. Nisqually Delta is a saltwater wetlands at the southern edge of Puget Sound. It is a place with a confluence of salt water and fresh; a place with a low, wide terrain and tide gentle enough to smooth and not erode the mud flats. It is a place where I expect to see birds: long-legged waders, cedar waxwings, red-tail hawks.

I have come to the Delta today to keep a promise I made to a Buddhist teacher of mine. This teacher is small and radiant, her eyes brimming with compassion and joy. The first time I was in her presence, I wanted to know how to live with all the suffering in our world without closing my heart. Sixty other people were there, many with the same question. We sat on the floor of an octagonal room. It was mid-summer. Sunlight poured in through a round skylight in the roof. There was a vase of flowers, the smell of lilies, the pure note of a Tibetan bell. That first time, my teacher said it was essential to express our grief for the planet; that until we can truly grieve we cannot fully feel or enact our love. She said that pain for the world comes from our caring, and in this way, it is a spiritual gift. I cried all weekend.

When I returned home, my heart felt as if it had been swept free of debris.

The next time I was with her, my teacher and I walked in the woods. She asked me about my life, those aspects of my life that had shaped my decision to seek her counsel, the nicks and bruises we all bear from the experience of living, the stories of loss. I told her of my father's environmental work, about his disillusionment and cynicism about the future, about my early fear of nuclear war. I told her about my love of the natural world, about the decades I lived in despair.

As I spoke, she leaned towards me and kissed the place on my left cheek where a single tear had fallen. "Remember," she said. "No matter what happens in the world, nothing can take away your capacity to love."

And now, five years later, those words return to me.

It is September 11, 2001, two hours after the towers of the World Trade Center collapsed. One hundred ten stories. Thousands of lives. Collapsed. Earlier this morning as I watched the reports on television, I experienced incredulity, shock and horror but the longer I watched, the more numb I became, the more separate from the pulse of life. When I asked myself what was required of me at this moment of crisis—as a woman, a psychotherapist, a writer, how might I respond?—the answer was clear. All I can really do is love the world.

So, I have come to Nisqually Delta, a landscape I am familiar with, a landscape where it is easy to sink into the silence, to listen to patterns in the clouds, the wind stirring dry grass, the hungry slurping of the bog. Today, morning light slants golden through fifty-foot spruce and hemlock trees; a great-blue heron hunches on the packed sand of the Bay; the air smells of wet earth, salt water and decomposing leaves. I walk slowly, occasionally stopping to run my hand down the mossy trunk of a tree in exactly the same way I run my hand over the fine, red hair on Richard's chest. I take great gulps of salty air, retrieve a maple leaf edged with bronze, scan the wild roses for empty nests.

The last half-mile of the trail winds through wide, grassy terrain. It is here that I often encounter the oval pellets of owls or the remains of mice and rabbits, torn apart by the sharp beaks of hawks. Today, brittle stalks of thistle rise amidst acres of amber grass. Up ahead, a single bush of blooming yellow flowers catches my eye. As I approach, the bush thrums to life and dozens of sun-bright goldfinches rise in unison, one body of shimmering brilliance, one heart.

This is what I know about loving the world: it is what we fear and desire most. When we have the courage to love the world by paying attention to everything about a person or a place and its inhabitants, we feel more fragile. The absence of a single tree, a species, the hunger of children, the lives lost in the rubble of New York, breaks our heart open. But loving the world in this way also strengthens us by connecting us to everything. It is this connection that makes it possible to survive our grief and to experience a sense of responsibility to the earth.

To remember the victims of September 11th, our city held a memorial of flowers at the International Fountain in the Seattle Center. That weekend, a procession of people brought sunflowers, sprays of purple gladiolas, orange dahlias and wreaths of white roses to the site. The event was scheduled to last three hours but people kept coming. Thirty thousand people came, leaving the ground ankle deep in flowers.

I had spent the week scanning each morning's newspapers for stories that opened me, that I found life affirming, that engendered hope. I clung to those stories, rested in them. A few came from the New York Times obituaries where the tributes to those who had died spoke of love and lives lived well. Others came from a friend of Richard's who lived only blocks from Ground Zero. He and his wife and their two daughters made sandwiches for the rescue crews. In the course of a single day, they'd made two thousand. I was inspired, as well, by the Dalai Lama's message to look for causes instead of blame; and by the show of grief from around the world. I felt fortunate to have these images but they felt two-dimensional. I found that I wanted the flesh and blood and bones of other people, the smell of roses and sweat.

On Saturday, Richard and I parked our car in a crowded neighborhood and walked the half-mile to the Fountain. We held hands but neither of us spoke. All week, we had been touching each other more frequently, looking into each other's eyes in the way people do when they recognize the fragility of all they hold most dear. That day was warm enough that sweat gathered between the palms of our hands and some of the purple and white cosmos I was carrying began to wilt.

When we reached the Fountain, it seemed the whole world was there. Sikhs wearing blue turbans were there. Firemen in dress uniform. Parents hugging small children and dogs. A young girl, her dark hair held back from her face with two barrettes. The blue dome of the sky was also there. Seagulls. There were the leaves on the trees and the muted, golden light of autumn.

Standing on the periphery of so much grief, so much fear and confusion, I knew immediately how I wanted to enter. I wanted to descend the concrete stairs, paying attention to each person I passed. Hundreds of people circled the fountain in a kind of slow current. As I joined them, faces approached and disappeared, sunburnt noses, mascara-streaked cheeks, bearded chins, translucent ears. Some people walked side by side but many were in single file. There were painted toenails, grass-stained knees and the bunion on my own left foot, throbbing. I found it easy to walk slowly. Everyone walked slowly as if we had been stopped in our tracks. The closer to the fountain, the more crowded it became. Elbows knocked together. Shoulders touched. I smelled perfume, after-shave lotion and flowers. I saw lips moving as if in prayer, knees bending, tear-splattered eyeglasses, a Saint Francis medal resting on a freckled chest.

At one point, I came face-to-face with a man wearing a red tunic and carrying a large bouquet of flowers. We both stopped. I softened my gaze and drank in his face: smooth, brown skin; dark, watery eyes; a small nose that glistened with sweat. I reminded myself that I was looking at a person who had also witnessed those buildings fall; a person who knew we were preparing to go to war. His own body—or the body of someone he loved—could be destroyed in a terrorist attack. I held his gaze and let myself open to the pain he carried; not only the pain of current events but also the accumulated sorrows, the losses and loneliness, the scrapes and bruises that all lives contain. As I looked into his eyes, I felt how much I wanted him to be free of pain, how much I wanted him to experience joy.

The International Fountain that day was a place where you could be slow and grief-stricken and silent in the company of others who were similarly moved. It was not just a memorial to those who had died, a way of getting closer to them, of praying for them, it was also an expression of life and the strength of community. Individually, we all felt small and vulnerable, the face of our world forever changed, while within our bodies, our hearts thrummed with hope. Everything that had seemed jagged and broken the day before was softening and mending. The world's problems were not solved but we were no longer alone.

OF THE NORTHWEST WIND

Not far from my home is a small island, connected to the mainland by a narrow isthmus. It is a place of marsh wrens and cattails, a place of moss and sturdy oaks, a place where thousands of crows gather to roost each night. I like to walk there at dusk and listen to the secret language of these ebony birds. In their dissonant rattles, gargles and squeals, they recount the stories of their day.

I have come to believe that crows occupy a sacred place in our world. They settle among us to flourish on what we have discarded. They feast on food scraps in our trash bins, on garbage in our landfills, on candy wrappers and apple cores on the shoulder of the roads and on the flattened bodies of roadkill itself. In this way, crows seem to practice an ancient Buddhist teaching: never turning from the death and rotting guts of life. I did not always feel this way about crows. But in the last five years, the crows that have passed through my hands have taught me of their ways.

I recall my first encounter with crows. It was late May and nine green-blue eggs spotted with brown were brought to the rehabilitation center. These nine eggs formed the entire clutch of a northwestern crow, *Corvus caurinus*, a name meaning of the northwest wind. Placed on a thick layer of flannel sheets in an incubator, the eggs hatched within a week. I volunteered to spend Sunday afternoons feeding them.

In the wild, baby crows would be crowded into the center of a nest of twigs, lined with cedar bark, grasses and the hair of deer. But I found the orphaned crows in an incubator in three clay bowls lined with toilet paper and strips of flannel, their scrawny necks enfolding each other for warmth. Each bald body, with its bony head, blind eyes bulging behind blue-veined lids and prominent ear holes, looked as if it had fallen into life from a long-ago world.

When I opened the glass door of the incubator, all nine birds craned their gossamer necks skyward and gaped, their voices a choir of rattles and muted squawks. I had been told that the eyes of baby crows are the color of a clear, blue sea but no one had told me that the landscape of their inner mouth is deep crimson like the petal of a rose.

Reaching towards a single bird, I slid a syringe of formula down its throat and slowly pushed in the plunger, then removed the syringe and repeated the process. When the nestling was full, it drooped over the edge of the bowl, its heart beating in a slow pulse through the blue veins of its neck. I fed each nestling in this way then covered the incubator with a thick cloth to reduce the amount of unnatural lighting they received.

While they slept, I went outside, sat on the ground near a shady thicket and opened *The Encyclopedia of North American Birds*, a book left for me by the previous volunteer. I read that there are eighteen species of corvids that include ravens, crows, magpies and the Clark's nutcracker. I read that the fossils of corvids have been discovered in deposits laid down in Colorado twelve million years ago; that crows have the highest degree of intelligence among birds and that in captivity, they should be offered various meats, soaked grains, bread, fruit, vegetables, mealworms and other insects. But that information did not hold me; I was hungry for something deeper. As I sat in the dappled light of an alder, I wondered about the dreams of crows. I wondered if they dream about the world they inhabited before this one; perhaps it was a world with golden seas of grain and cobalt skies where the deep nights are guarded by three silver moons.

Over the next month as the crows' blue eyes opened, hollow indigo quills became the strong feathers of flight and dark bristles sprouted on the crowns of bald heads, I read everything the library had about ravens and crows. I sat in a dusty room with dozens of books spread around me on a long table. I read a children's book about the greed of Raven and another about Raven's generosity in sharing its food. I discovered that in England it was thought that to see a crow would ward off evil spirits but that in Wales, it was considered unlucky if a crow crossed your path. In some countries, I read, it was a bad omen to see two crows flying together while in other countries, this sign was thought to herald success. French peasants thought that bad priests became ravens and bad nuns became crows while many Native American tribes associated crows with the return of peace and abundance on earth.

I was struck by these images and the other stories I read where the raven is considered a trickster, a clown, a mischief-maker and a buffoon. These are stories that in different cultures and in different times, helped people make sense of the world. The stories reminded me how a simple thing can be made complex; how a simple thing can be given a variety of meanings by the human mind. I was also reminded of the power of story itself, of how the stories we tell ourselves, about each other and about the world, shape our experience and determine the actions we take.

In captivity, baby birds do not receive the nourishment of fresh air and sunlight like nestlings raised in the wild and this lack can weaken their immune system and make them vulnerable to disease. In mid-July, one of the nine crows we'd hatched from an egg contracted an eye infection. To prevent contagion, that bird was housed with ten other eye-infected crows in a low room the size of a child's playhouse. It was my job to care for those birds.

I entered the room on my knees. It was early morning. The wooden floor was strewn with mucousy excrement, dog food swollen with water and the browned edges of apple cores. The air was stale and smelled of rotting flesh. One crow lay stiffly on its back like a fallen soldier, a single dark feather clinging to its chest.

After the cawing and clacking of wings had stilled, I took in the condition of the sick crows. With eyes swollen and oozing, they hobbled about, blindly lilting from side to side. Some had also been injured in collisions with cars or dogs and their broken feet or legs were held in place by red gauze and strong, white tape. In the face of their brokenness, I was drawn to speak of their wholeness so I began to whisper strands of a creation story I'd read. I told the crows that in the beginning of time, it was one of them—transformed into a spruce needle—that was swallowed by a dark haired woman who gave birth to a boy. This boy, I said, took the golden orb of the sun from beneath a blanket and rolled it outside. Once outside, the boy became Crow again and flew up to return the sun to the sky. It was you, I told the crows, who gave the earth its rivers of light.

I began feeding the crows. Some were ravenous and gaped easily. Others needed light stroking to the neck or my hand mimicking the open beak of a parent bird. Still others were weak and confused, the sharp edge of their breastbone visible. I lifted those frail ones onto my lap and with feather-light fingers caressed the violet gloss of their dark wings.

While I attended to the other crows, the nestling I cared for earlier in the summer perched on my knee. He was similar to the other crows but I recognized him by a certain soft murmuring that had always been his way. He murmured to me then, and I understood how he yearned for the world outside of these walls, the world he had glimpsed only from behind the smooth, thin shell of an egg. He yearned to hear the music of the breeze and the hum of the crickets, yearned to soar on those vast rivers of light. As I listened to him, I laid a finger between his oozing eyes, ran my hand down his dark back. I, too, hoped he lived to see the world whole.

When the hunger of the crows was satiated, I began the task of cleaning their room. I lifted the body of the dead crow, plucked the loose feather from its chest and wrapped it in a soft, white cloth. As many of the crows slept, I removed the debris from the room and washed down the walls. I emptied the bowls, drew fresh water and placed fragrant spruce boughs on the floor. The nestling leaned sleepily into another bird: black claws holding tight to his perch; wild, black wings folded around him like a cloak. If it is God that opens our heart, then this is what God looks like. This dark face, those blue eyes, the crimson landscape of that mouth.

BENEDICTION

for Valerie

AT FOUR IN THE MORNING, THE WILDLIFE center is nearly silent, even the nocturnal animals are asleep. Winding your way through a thicket of alder, oak fern, rhododendron and Oregon grape, you may not hear a sound. By six in the morning, steam rises from the cedar bark path and the woods are shot through with light. A few sleepy volunteers straggle in from the parking lot holding steaming cups of coffee or tea. By seven o'clock on any summer morning, a cacophony of trills and whistles rise like a cloud through the dense canopy of leaves. I have loved those sounds, the earth's generous invocation of day.

After four years of such mornings, it has become my preference to work alone. The quiet, the lack of conversation with other volunteers, allows me to move in time with the birds' rhythms, to be still enough that I am able to intuit their needs. Some birds seem to require that I remember my place as separate from them. Others like the swallows, crows and an occasional chickadee or wren, prefer to perch on my arms or nestle into my hair.

Aside from the obvious rewards of this work such as watching an evening grosbeak recover from a virus or a robin's broken foot mend, there have been others. In my summers at HOWL, I have come to understand that what I am calling hope is a deep attention to whatever is before me, a willingness to move towards life. Whether I am feeding insects to a willow flycatcher, cleaning cages or replenishing the supply of food; when I bring my entire self to the task, hope inhabits me. Delicate. Fluttering. Real. I believe in these moments. And I believe all of life can be lived in this way. The birds, and my relationship with Valerie, taught me this is so.

Valerie had already been diagnosed with leukemia when we met. I became involved in her life at the request of a mutual friend who was working in Sri Lanka at the time. The friend told me that Valerie had undergone chemotherapy in New York City and had come to Seattle for radiation treatment and a bone marrow transplant. The friend asked if I would meet Valerie and her husband who had no other family or friends in the Pacific Northwest. She suggested I might provide counseling or support of some kind or help them get acquainted with a strange city. I'd been around sickness and death before and I knew it required a certain presence. At the time, I felt reluctant to be that engaged, especially with a stranger. But my friend had nurtured me during a difficult time and to reciprocate in this way felt intuitively right.

Valerie was long-limbed, graceful, and warm in the immediately intimate way of the French. She had a regal manner and radiant eyes. Her skin was tawny as if she'd spent the last week in the sun and her hair—just growing in after chemotherapy—was thick and coarse and wavy. That first day, she and her husband sat across from me at a café. The room, filled with winter sunlight, was empty except for us. It was mid-afternoon and the ten or twelve other tables, were set with linen napkins, silverware and long-stemmed glasses. There were candles on each table and a single yellow rose.

While Valerie chewed her pizza and salad and sipped at her tea, she told me about being in Paris at Christmas. She spoke of coming down with what felt like a bout of flu, about the malaise and weakness that had lingered for weeks, about the leukemia diagnosis and the shock. She was matter-of-fact in this telling, without complaint.

I asked about her prognosis.

When she met my gaze, her eyes lacked any trace of hesitation or fear. "The statistics say my chances of survival are slim," she said. She looked towards her husband and ran an index finger slowly down the line of his jaw. "But we've decided to be hopeful. I'm young. In good shape. Who knows what can happen."

Valerie's words reminded me of what my Buddhist teacher had said when I'd asked her about hope. "My hope," she'd told me, "comes from the nature of living systems." She said that because everything from an atom to a galaxy is connected, we can't know all the influences each will have on the others; that we make a mistake believing that from what we know we can predict everything. As my teacher often did, she'd told me a story. She spoke of how hydrogen and oxygen combine to make water. "There is nothing in what we know of either hydrogen or oxygen," she'd said, "that predicts the physical qualities of what they create." Over the years I'd sat with her, she'd told me this again and again until the cells of my body understood that no one could predict the consequences of even the smallest action taken on behalf of life. It's in the relationship of one thing to another that the unforeseeable can arise.

I asked Valerie what she wanted from me in the next few weeks.

She gazed out the window and took her time answering as if weighing which of her immediate needs I might meet. "A few visits in the hospital would be nice," she said. "And some gourmet cooking magazines."

The sun was still shining the following week when I visited Valerie for the first time. Outside her hospital window, there was pale blue sky and traffic streaming across the University Bridge. There were the bare branches of oak trees on Capitol Hill and Mount Rainier, a massive guardian in the distance. Inside her room, there were greeting cards from friends in Paris, an arrangement of silk flowers and a stuffed bear with a red plastic heart.

I sat down on the end of Valerie's bed and while a nurse drew a vial of blood from her arm, I massaged her legs and feet. The idea of massaging her had surfaced in me when we'd embraced at the end of our first meeting. I had felt the tension she was carrying in her body and it had occurred to me then, that touch was a simple thing I could offer, a tangible way to lessen her pain. When I mentioned this idea to Valerie she was thrilled. She said her body had been aching for weeks and she had been missing her masseur in New York.

Valerie's skin was warm under the palm of my hand and as silky and smooth as the lotion I'd brought. As I massaged her, she entertained me with stories from her childhood. She told me about a grandmother that she had loved who lived a simple life in southern France. She spoke of the woods surrounding her grandmother's cottage and of the rice pudding baked for hours on a wood-burning stove. I knew that Valerie was afraid but she didn't speak of her illness that day, or of the bone marrow transplant taking place the following morning. Instead she spoke of life, of the beaches on Fire Island, of good friends and laughter and food, of being in love with her husband and of good sex on warm nights between cool cotton sheets. She talked to me in this way for some time until her eyes began to droop and she fell asleep, her head leaning against the crook of one arm.

I looked at Valerie, at her rosy lips, slightly parted; at her eyelids, blue-veined like a baby bird; at the gentle rise and fall of her chest. Here was a woman, twenty years younger than I was, facing a life-threatening disease. Anyone would have understood if she'd felt despairing, if she'd closed down to life and turned away from anything that reeked of hope. But she hadn't. Instead, she let hope rise in her and collect around the smallest details of her day. The phone call from France she met with exuberance. The bald eagle soaring by her window. Her daily walks down the florescent-lit corridor, bags of IV fluids trailing behind her on silver wheels. I wanted hope to live in me that way. And it did, most of the time. But if I were facing my own death, would I continue to reach for life in all its clacking, creaking, buzzing, humming forms? Or would hope elude me, driven away by resignation, bitterness or fear?

A week after the transplant, the blue flannel sky was still cloudless and the southern-facing window in Valerie's room was bright with reflected light. Nurses wandered in and out of the room with glasses of chipped ice, wool blankets, thermometers and blood pressure cuffs. Soft voices drifted in from the hallway as I sat on the end of Valerie's bed. Even though her hair had fallen out since I'd last seen her and she'd had a few days of nausea and fatigue, she still exuded warmth and optimism, still welcomed me with a huge smile. That day, I massaged the tender skin behind her knees, the muscles of her calves, slender like the neck of a swan, the high arch of each foot, the webbed skin between her toes. We didn't talk much and after a while, Valerie's eyelids slid shut and her limbs went limp in my hands. Her husband had gone out for coffee when I arrived and the quiet in the room, the warmth, drew me into a kind of reverie in which the outside world—with its hurry and noise—fell away. There was only the shaft of sunlight on the bed, the slip of melting ice, the stack of unread magazines on the floor. There was the smell of alcohol in the room and the faint scent of vanilla rising from Valerie's skin. I think it was the quality of attention I brought to Valerie's body combined with her openness and vulnerability that made these moments possible. Whatever it was, these were the times I came to cherish most: being with her in this very quiet way.

Because of her compromised immune system, Valerie was not allowed to have flowers or living plants in her room so I became the landscape she noticed. Each time I arrived at her room with gourmet cooking magazines, rice pudding or new massage oil, she insisted I turn round and round, so she could see the clothes I wore. When I did, she exclaimed in her lilting French accent and kissed the air with her glossy lips. At first, her attention made me self-conscious but later, I began to dress for her, selecting each outfit with her delight in mind. I wore emerald green velvet pants with maroon silk scarves wrapped around my shoulders. I dyed my hair red, wore vermilion lipstick and mauve polish on my toes. I gave myself to her in this way just as her body had given itself to my touch. I became her bird of paradise, the vase of flowers entering her room, a red-winged blackbird lifting its wings in flight.

Four weeks after the transplant, Valerie was released. She had always loved to walk, but after the confinement of the hospital, she couldn't seem to walk enough. She walked everyday, moving through the city streets, the wind stinging her skin, the fresh air seeping into her pores. One day, she and I walked along Elliott Bay. We walked for hours. It was March, a day of bitter winds. The sky was gray and low and heavy with rain. We walked holding hands, Valerie's palm sweaty against mine. There was the smell of seaweed as we walked, and wet earth. We saw the sleek head of a seal, a white-crowned sparrow, a single crocus poking up through frozen ground. At one point, it started to rain so hard that we huddled together under a tree, heads bent low, faces bright with laugher and cold.

Some thought it was foolish for Valerie to walk in wind and rain, exposed to all the elements, with no immune system at all. But she was alive and she wanted to be surrounded by the sheer abundance of life, to be immersed in the living pulse of each day. I admired her for that. Isn't that the challenge we all face: how to stay engaged when life seems dangerous or uncertain? In the face of war, environmental disaster, the threat of terrorist attacks, do we cloister ourselves and create the pretense of safety? Or do we do what our heart wants: open our body to smell and taste and touch it all?

When Valerie was readmitted to the hospital with a lung infection, spring was at its most beautiful. It spilled onto all the sidewalks and grassy areas of the city, and burst with fragrance. The sky was robins egg blue and there were cherry blossoms, clusters of purple wisteria and magnolias as round as a dinner plate. The day after her readmission, Valerie's father and three closest friends arrived from Paris. The mood of that day was celebratory. The pain medication Valerie was given made her ebullient. It was a reunion of friends. There were stories of Valerie as a young girl translated into English for me. Valerie was all hand gestures and kisses. We laughed loudly and occasionally fell into fits of giggling that made us hold our stomachs and fall over on the bed.

But the next day, Valerie was exhausted. In the visitor's lounge, her husband told me the results of the chest x-ray were not good. The infection had spread. Her lung capacity was diminishing. The doctor had said she would not leave the hospital alive. I asked John what he thought happened after death. He said his ideas about this were always changing, but he didn't think there was another world after this one. It was more that people lived on in our memories of them, he said, as love, in our heart. He asked what I believed. I told him I thought that at death what is essential about each of us becomes part of everything. "Only the body dies," I said. "Everything else remains."

The blue sky continued but for the rest of the week, the shades in Valerie's room were drawn. The six of us sat around her bed. We took turns feeding her ice chips, putting gloss on her lips, holding her hands. Her feet and ankles were too swollen to massage, so I stroked her head, her forehead, and her arms. There was the hiss of oxygen and nurses coming in and out of the room. It was a tender, gentle time.

One afternoon, I was alone with Valerie. She was lying under two blankets but she spoke of being unable to get warm. I massaged her shoulders and the soles of her feet. But even then, she said she felt no warmer. At one point, I crawled into bed with her and wrapped my body around hers trying to absorb the cold.

It was so peaceful lying next to her. There was the silence in the room and outside the window, the soft glow of apricot light. As I held her body in my arms, I felt how her chest and belly were collapsing in on themselves. Her legs and arms were more bone than flesh. Under my hands, she was shrinking, drawing towards her center, and I found myself reminded of how stars die.

When death comes for a star, it shrinks, draws into itself, expends less energy in radiance and pouring out and more energy towards going in. A dying star doesn't wink out and disappear, it gives itself back to the universe as dust. Nothing is lost. Our bodies, the very earth we live on, are nothing more than the dust of ancient stars. I believe this is what the Old Testament meant by the phrase we come from dust and unto dust we shall return. As a child, I was frightened by this idea because it meant the dissolution of everything I held most dear. But lying next to Valerie, I understood those words as a message of continuation. Life gives itself back to its beginnings. Everything a circle.

Dusk arrives at the wildlife center and the thrush offers its last spiraling benediction to the canopy of leaves. The work of the day is complete and silence descends, settling quietly into the heart. This is a moment I believe in, this divide between day and night, when Earth gathers everything back to herself. It is a moment when I am reminded that what was essential about Valerie is inherent in all of life. What we shared can be recalled when I touch wing or fin or paw. Her love and warmth, the quiet between us, even her voice are the sunlight on water, the wind through aspen leaves, the whisper of wings taking flight.

ACKNOWLEDGMENTS

I COULD NOT HAVE WRITTEN THIS BOOK WITHOUT the support and guidance of many people. At the top of that list must be my parents, Ray and Jane Grob, who not only gave me life but also introduced me to the natural world, awakened my love of birds and opened our home to an array of wild creatures. Thank you. I will always be grateful to my mentor, Joanna Macy, who taught me to let my heart break open so it could hold the whole world. And to Marilyn Strong and Jerry Wenstrom who brought me to a threshold and accompanied me across. My writing teacher, Brenda Peterson, was unwavering in her belief and support. Her generosity of spirit is equal to her editorial skill. I want to acknowledge the women in the Monday night writing group: Catherine Johnson, Trish Maharan, Connie Feutz, Irene Svete, Laura Foreman, Rebekka Stahl, Gail Hudson and Suzanne Edison. I am grateful to you for enduring draft after miserable draft of these stories. Our conversations kept me honest and kept the writing moving forward. Two of them in particular became my dear companions: Trish Maharan and Gail Hudson. To you, I am devoted. I want to acknowledge the generosity of Dee Hein, who offered not only friendship but also a place of solitude on Orcas Island. Several editors along the way believed in my work. Warren Schlesinger of OSU Press read the original manuscript and his astute question had me reverse course. Linda Gunnarson at Sierra Press and Mary Ann Naples at the Literary Agency believed in my stories and provided editorial wisdom that helped me craft the manuscript. To them, I owe a debt of thanks. Lastly, I would like to express the deepest gratitude to my husband, Richard Chadek, who lived these stories with me. Thank you for giving me the stars.

978-0-595-41558-8
0-595-41558-X

Printed in the United States
67970LVS00002BA/7-15